THE PINK

THE PINK

JARED SCHICKLING

BLAZEVOX[BOOKS]
Buffalo, New York

publisher of weird little books

BlazeVOX [books]

blazevox.org

BlazeVOX

"the Child-Made-Man-Woman is"

all incidents depicted in this book occurred

the 50%:

THE PINK

4321

Plastic flesh squat on the ground spits its paper! It chews knowing what to
do from without! Electricity's weaving it!

To satellites and back! Bits: Flagged! Each house on the street of thirty
houses! Spitting its own trees!

Some more than others! Some not at all!

Power lines! lashed to boards bolted a species of limb snapping one night
through gusting minor storms

Electricity shines. Screen. Giving it beer. Keys tap.

A jar of pencils is useless. Realize these two together. Organ forgotten.

To see that you see. Pulled the current from the ether.

Print.

Revised!

bee bay
yoo hoo
nothing to be done

Brought up off and on by continuously
absent people, who blames them
one barefoot in the grass to the one
whose small shoes crossed his toes permanently

As his man he'd punch the door which
gave way or shattered, who blames him
who'd blame her for himself
pulling it from her

stomach who'd say nothing about the one
no one knows, who blames her
her own dad shipped it off well before
they'd marry move

on I am a man I'll do nothing
but listen, or wait to hear it
because as their boy I knew
how they blamed things

Voice from her begins
not to speak, it spills
another's breast
telekinesis, more laundry

What it says
to who is hers
coconut geyser   man
man if we could taste you   if we could taste you

I was an accident

Finding myself
positions unfamiliar
filling its drawers

Speak, baby, speak—and under my adult life, straighten the dull people,
shrieking high and sour, following, without dirtying feet, a harder earth,
underneath my history.

,—and upon my hands

Drop a task that doesn't outward seep. I lose the path in these open ears.
Adulthood's heavy grief, or articulate ecstasies and hopes, mature,
clarifying words,

.—cosmetic peace, addled

consistent secret, laughs with a smoke, on laughing days, in the night,
procrastinate—follow her already.

Loud was the wild within—speak, baby, speak

At night, at my computer

Some open air without small shoes
When all but children raise voices:
Some walled space where we
Will never sit apart
Or, complex penpal, you my head
Out of gross isolation will offer:
A poor night factory, worst least, *
Without a sound torn from the walls
Or enough within them;
A bothersome room and there to sweep
Or say to its wordless wild
That you drip;
Or bothersome here to sit on chairs
To hear the scurrying beneath you;
A peace within this city,
Its frowning mouth far from its air,
Its safe cascade,
A sprouting kite, a laughing smell,
Its sad sheep underfluid
Or bleating as it dries:
None of that will appear musty new,
Or a young bar was blooming yesterday;
I stuck out, and wore, the common, brains
Or hid my more familiar person.
A bed approached, bugs in a swamp,
At last stops up your parent's mill;
Naturally not! them adults nevertheless
Wouldn't announce this to a yard!
Above a lamb—I never was here—
Your flesh ear graced a rock

That you will yet work,
Or it couldn't watch to listen or hear:
"We are close to Psyche"

I

born

spitting up

1: BABE WESTERN

Learntoheadouts
idebymys
elfmaynotmeetits
tilltherea
resuch
whoseethems
elvesremystery
maybethiss
kinofalls
wept.

B TO ME

You've suckled at her nipple.
You've tasted it now.
Go to sleep.

followed

here

inside

2: BREADWINNER

Assumed escaped mutually
assured devastation to
flee like squirrels.

3:

Chimay. And so this is the beginning of my love
to you. Thanks to you,

have not written one of these in a long time. Thanks to you
while you were on vacation

with Beatrice never got your turkey
with Beatrice, trashed the house. It's as if becoming

your kid again.
Pères Trappistes!

o great cow

being

flies

4:

Through her undeveloped cerebral cortex has
developed to a point she
can remember much she's not
good at remembering
food and all that I
had tried to write you something sentimental.

It created

Knots in
my back

(obviously—look at me!
)

5: Statement from a Novelist

Fatal bait for ants—idea—UFOs apparently (key word) releasing an
element or fact (or some thing) into the atmosphere which ~~becomes~~ proves
something irresistibly to all (human)(-ish) beings, ~~and~~ but to their demise
(choice of ending?)(in sum, 4), it don't need characters yet. It needs an
organizer, binding together, slowly in the detail, but eventually, in *one*
place, stage direction & all, the total plurality in all this detailed
complexity. How to ~~bring~~ find each of these—once it has this structure, or
cont(r)act, then the characters are free to develop themselves against the
center of the ~~fate~~ home erected for them & ~~though I~~ it's here, outside, that
they'll see how it ends.

II

all incidents occurred in this book

breadwinner

buried moistening flower death

blooming silk dissipated landscape

cloud body modulate

down only aftermath casket

refined up recline parties

system parks interned chrysalis

hot thickening land

load gas endlessness craving

blooming mountain pants cool

deliberate hand freeing struggle

Former Tenant
Day Erogenous

There is a zone you go
to
when you work
with hands, you lay at night under fans
fanning crotch
area, "all things matter
to themselves," spoke
she, but not her words, not really, "therefore
I'm an atheist" & here's the rub (repeating
my work) the only way for something to be interesting
is to become something else
—wherefore drywall—ideas
wherefore sheetrock paint and tools, & a pornographic magazine
("No Lie") left behind
as if intentionally, a portion of the ceiling and the kitchen sink
I have removed; a dumpster today on the side of the house; "begin
again
whatever, look at those ants, (flip the page,) they're in the pool all
day
I'm jealous; I am not the people.
I am inside and outside and inside and outside.
I would take your fantasy away & give you fresher produce like I
will
wash your hands for you.
I know this because I had to drop the toilet onto your foot
until its toes do not clench
at crayons. You always have to, had to, end, see.

FROST ON MORNING'S LONG WINDOWED SHADOW'S ON SPLITTING
DECK'S DIRT'S MIXING RECYCLABLE RUBBER RAINED FROM THE
FIRE'S ON PLASTIC YELLOW BUCKET'S WEEDY YARD FENCED ROUND
WITH PIKES' PAINTED OTHER SIDE'S INVISIBLE WOODS' SHADOW'S
ALSO ON RUBBER'S RAIN

Brown and dried tomatoes
leaves green fruit left.

Chimp
a wash the hands
for it

Peeled a dipstick early
dropped a toilet

On the foot the
toes

are in it back
to wiping

On Perpetual Bliss

skin
climate

sublime

property
critical point   ~~with a~~
as attractor thus displays   ~~an~~

scale-invariance
at critical point   ~~the~~
phase

transition no need yr
tuning controls   ~~to precise~~
values precise

point of that noise

Riddle and a Mugging
Passerine (order), Tit (family)

A traveler passed through, dismissing for you
its feathers, beak, even a black bib; of course you'd still wonder;
The feathers, and you, quick;
The beak you emptied, but it fibbed, so you went back in.

Outside you, bibs, & a squeak, uproots you
play me, hello, crests we should
have to take off, joy already divides us,
You'd even go back; so a whole world would know

@ my computer

Green's first flight

Pink   over picket fence

Fresh   clear was my pattern heard

Clear   fresh threads through air

Under   refreshing sky alive

Where   around me would brim & form

Slavishly   pink here

Upon   stumbled

Almost   my well-lubed life stopped

Many   will perform me a product

Of   a muscle who jumped in skins of my living

Many   will perform me the spectral beings

And   still the selfless acting

The   things bone

Special   seed torn bearing pink

Pink   on the greenhouse, bone & seed

bones   went moist bad

acting,   spray it *   * minor drought, 2012

                       thought without its flower knew

It   wasn't ignorant; so then to a sky would bound

Gasps   to a head were delivered

Gasps   breaths, as the desiccations order

Absorbed   jumped into brittle seeds

And   petals

What   hadn't spread it hasn't possibly lived!

The   mind to keep its mind was its choice.

la lin da
ma ni ta
que tiene el
be bé

qué lin da
qué bel la
qué bo ni
ta es

the pink, B:

Never will there be a man from whom earth will have taken all gods.

Never will he be going without the gods from the many-legged forest when a wild creature will be kept, or he will soil himself here, outside the blurred arroyo.

A devotee, of course, spoke for me, because gods had a soft spot for demanding, even in the desert, I will with difficulty escape from safety.

One will play alone, or hate itself, without its brain, or a young devotee will go in, hunted as the beggar.

And from there she will come, or where she will have gone tomorrow he will have performed it, or will have heard, why shouldn't I have kept a live body from the guilty girl that will have ever healed no one.

Where she will have come, he will have the big head taken from him, or will have asked him to save it, or will have taken his brain or ear from him, or snatching itself from under the table, or where he will have felt a young woman going, he will have heard from a girl, stand up on your yard, and release my nakedness from me.

A queen's daughter will have departed here the long contraction shorter, or where she will have actualized her father, or will have scrutinized him because he will have at last been dead.

Uh huh, he will have asserted, being lost was rather not quick, or you know what you did to the familiar sea when you were acknowledged.

She will have gone from a dungeon upon which her father will have been
released, or it will have been so low, she will have demanded the rope
(and harness) that would not have stopped shy of the least bottom.

Before she will have spelunked the first time, or will have come her mother,
or will have allowed herself to pronounce herself the familiar prey, or will
have looked around and demanded that she could not have taken her usage

Two of every animal and spirit or less will have sauntered outside a broken
hoop in their own passing time, or unworthy prey will have escaped

Then a queen will have known a tinge of sadness away from that, or asked
if none of her enemies would have fasted without her yesterday, or unmade
one instance of hunger.

So much will she have deformed an expectation once a maiden will have
finished, or heard, my iniquity, they died sorrowfully there, so we all knew
a king dying near a dungeon.

And from here she will have brought or given a cat without a silver chain,
or will have heard, this was a beauty, or will have been the effect of a dead
fire taken, or those a cat will have been coaxed into spitting up after a
sound from no one, once ice will have been swallowed into its mouth.

Before which prey will have heard no more or will have heard, mother, why
didn't I hear a lord that will have ruined you not forcibly or that will have
beforehand given life to me, and so will have done me, since his own death
will have not been depended on.

But a queen received one lord or one waiting-maid from out of her keep,
where nothing echoes, having fetched the king or taken him from a lowly
plate.

Here is your mother
in this bottle. Here is the rocking chair
you won't remember.

and not even this, B:

One day will be the woman who is passive. That will do what her father will demand. For some reason or other the workplace will suffer much from her. Or keep her from becoming healthy. Or her visitors will not be able to do her harm. Or after a long time. She will stand on her cradle.

Where she will be lifted out. Once so much of it is wadded around her. Bit by bit she will happen. Going inward. Where her leg would bend for the first time. Or will reflex and expand. Where it will take her out they will be full of purpose despite it.

Before her mother. That one. Will be free to come from her cradle. Or from legs be struck without a bone. She must do this. And he should probably be there. As before eternity. A girl lives life into the air.

IV

name

@

1:

Is blood spilled
or blood circulating
the circulation of blood spilling or
is "good"
troublesome
especially before
we even decide
what "life" meant?

Soft by a small city dwelt a cook with her husband, who had many
children, including a big boy of many years old. They were so rich,
however, that they started to make their own bread, and just so they could
feed each other. Many nights the cook went out with glee to her fun in the
kitchen, and while she was cooking food, slowly there dawned within her a
short, repulsive, middle-aged man with big toes sticking out of the opened
ends of his shoes, covered in hair. He didn't say anything, but thought, "I
am who you think I am. You are rich and you need nothing, take your boy
from his dad, I will give him to you and you can be his mother and don't
worry, you won't have to care about him." The cook disobeyed, kept her
child for him, and took him from the old man, who left alone without him.

3:

There used to be a young man who had many large parents—[he hated them with every bit of himself]. One day he decided, I would like to leave the city and travel and find some new clothes, just like these, given to me, but I don't know where to begin. I could use some advice. The boy felt old. So he telephoned each of his parents, and after each excuse he finally heard, son, you may not come in here, open yourself to this, little lamb, we left it specifically for you, if you let it get away, you will go hungry—[skin, hair, and everything]. Such a gift is rare you are mistaken—[lips loose on white heads]. Then the old man said, dear dad. Don't worry. I won't take bad care of myself. This young one burped. That got them a laugh.

Blood? the Spirit

The uncertain mom had two daughters, the younger of whom was smart and could neither forget nor misunderstand anything, at all, but the older one was dumb and unreasonable. She had done next to nothing, at all, so that when someone saw her, they could say, "here is a lady who's received the calm of her mother." Whenever nothing was to be initiated, in the evening, around the house, as this was often her mother's strategy, the younger was allowed to do nothing at all that she wanted, and if her mother put her in the corner, especially if it was early—that is, in the night—and the blocked way followed into the cradle, or such happy places, she'd wonder, "I see, mother, but what do you want? I will go there, it makes me happy." For she was. And when creaking was heard from the carpet in the chilly mornings making a spirit sleep, the other daughter would also hear it: "I will go there, it makes me happy." At such times, when the older one felt safely alone, she practiced her art of seeing what neither saw. "She'll never say it makes me sad—it's always I'm happy, I'm happy." Spoke she. "This alone will make us happy."

5:

Here she fared poorly, starved of vegetables, and of milk, and her skin was almost plastic, and a big man ignored her. And once she was young again, he heard from her: "Dear sir, I have made this trip, done these deeds, so release from your protection this one lock to what is beneath you. Feel free to do anything you want with it, and just so I am a bit reluctant, but you obviously cannot open it. Take care in choosing, lest you be happy." The man lied saying he would release it, and when she had come, he'd already accepted that he could not part with it. Not once had he even tried to open it, though he'd rubbed it, worn it, thrown it, licked it, bit it, smelled it, he'd even put the tiny hole to his ear (more than once), and though he could not remember how he'd come by it, with this lock he'd found a way to accomplish the whole spectrum of sensation. And though new ideas kept springing into his head, eventually he'd forgotten his desire to see and feel that slow click, or whatever he'd imagined would, come from his fingertips. He said to the woman, "I will open it one day, just you watch, here in this opening, watch." "Ok," said the woman, "that would be nice. I only ask that you do in fact open it, and in doing it, this time, give it back and be happy." Once she'd turned around, to wait, he thought, "now I am quite alone, I could peep in, if I do, no one will know," and when he looked, the lock pulsed, he was so surprised that just before he lost it with his foot he somehow slowly as he realized was proffering it aloft with his thumb and forefinger. He opened his eyes and she was looking at it. She stayed there a while, looking at it. Then she touched it. Eight of her digits gently touched the wrought iron, stiffly quivering, curling around it, and as they did, one by one, he simply accepted it, though he felt pale, and he shrank a little. He felt slow relief. As if he'd done this before. He straightened himself, and took one step forward. He clicked his heels. But his backbone would not quit him as two of his digits were still pinching at the lock, from beneath it, as if to bring it to his nose.

V

"bee bay"
"yoo hoo"

court got
an affliction   i.e. fucked

lidocaine patched
back lifted

inside voice
enters plea

Venus: balled
gases, hypothetical
inside

“bee bay”
“yoo hoo”

yeah i'd like to get together soon. tis the season. i'm preoccupied come
night time, in the midst of a learning curve that seems to be magically just
happening. don't want to interrupt it. took a walk for a few miles through
the swamps last night, pitch black by the time we got back, the
sunset/twilight last for an hour. otters and geese everywhere. went out to
keg creek the other day, it was very chilly near the water, took b, sat for a
while and then went back to the orchard and took a nap together in the
sun with a chainsaw buzzing in the background. francine jumped out my
office window the other night while we were sleeping. completely my fault
and terrifying to find some kind neighbor had brought her back and put
her inside the front entryway. this spring is phenomenal. have you been
watching venus and jupiter? they were like floodlights in the sky last
night. they've been doing loops around each other. we should take a walk
on the towpath or something; you bring buddha and i'll bring b, we bought
a stroller that's good for bumpy terrain.

the genetic origin of the sexes is a shrunken, mutated x
at night, at my computer

Caused by love or caused by learning to hate
Caused by pleasures in being born
Less than pleasures in not being born,
I'll hear me: "We'll learn from her
Image." Of course. We will or won't. And she ages
A little unlike us,
Epoch of epochs.

Often she did everything in her home
And still was celebrated: He heard her,
With others at a full garden,
Drinking with the charade of a wild domesticate.
I listened to her, join me
As she joined with herself,
Organic, disorder.
I listened to her, or keep your body beneath you
She saw him; I saw her.

"bee bay"
"yoo hoo"

had to write that, B (50%):

a narrative dictates it, for one.
the other is that
look out for it
she gets you.
seriously.

Beatrice
Wren
me
sired by
her
Mollie

an accident

"bee bay" – "black-capped chickadee"
was "yoo hoo"
easy to see

BM: * *buried* *moistening* * drought, 2012 she just brought me buttered
toast!

    blooming *silk*

    cloud *body* *modulate*

    down   *aftermath*

    refined   *recline*

    system   *interned* *chrysalis*

    hot

    load   *craving*

    blooming   *cool*

    deliberate   *struggle*

Jared Schickling's other books of poetry are *Aurora, submissions, O, Zero's Blooming Excursion,* and *t&u& lash your nipples to a post history is gorgeous* (BlazeVOX [books], 2007-11). Current projects include a prequel to *The Pink*, "(pietà: Ramona's Private Jest.)," a work of poetics, "The Paranoid Arrow: Studies in that American Fiction," and occasional translations of passages from Moroccan poet Abdellatif Laâbi's *L'automne promet*. He likes *1913: a journal of forms; The Associative Press; Bombay Gin; Circumference: Poetry in Translation; ecopoetics; ditch, the poetry that matters; Exquisite Corpse; Interim Magazine; Jacket; kadar koli; Literary Imagination; Little Red Leaves; Omnia Vanitas Review: A Journal of Literary Erotica; Otoliths; Sous les Pavés; SpringGun; unarmed journal; We Are So Happy to Know Something; Word For/Word: a journal of new writing* and more. In 2006 he got a *KNOCK* Ecoliterature / Green Art prize in poetry. He is a founding editor of Delete Press and *eccolinguistics,* and he serves on the editorial board of *Reconfigurations: A Journal for Poetics and Poetry / Literature and Culture*. He teaches English at a community college and lives near Buffalo, NY.

Made in the USA
Monee, IL
07 July 2026

56551618R00049